FOURSQUARE

21 Days of Prayer + Fasting 2025
Family Moments

SPIRIT-Filled PRAYER

What's INSIDE

with the whole family

"And pray in the Spirit on all occasions with all kinds of prayers and requests. With this in mind, be alert and always keep on praying for all the Lord's people."
—Eph. 6:18 (NIV)

The words Paul shares in Ephesians 6:18 are both our prayer and commission for your family as you step into 21 Days of Prayer + Fasting 2025. We pray that your next 21 days will be marked by praying in the Spirit on all occasions with all kinds of prayers and requests, that you will be alert, and that you will always keep on praying for all the Lord's people.

As you set aside time and embrace this opportunity to connect as a family, let's trust the Holy Spirit to guide and speak. The beauty of focusing on Spirit-filled prayer is the understanding that the Holy Spirit is our Teacher. He is ready to lead your family and speak to every family member of any age! The Family Moments found in this book are designed to support you along the way. They include practical activities and conversations to help get you started.

The instructions we find in Ephesians 6:18 follow the call to put on the armor of God. There is a very real spiritual battle for the hearts and minds of our children and families. The Holy Spirit testifies to the victory we have in Jesus, and we have the privilege of engaging in God's kingdom work with prayer and, in turn, being filled with His power.

We recognize there are so many things competing for your family's time and attention. We ask you to prayerfully ask yourself: "What is one faith habit we can start as a family?"

If helpful, we've included blessing prayers for each of the 21 days. Blessings can be prayers of commission, Bible verses or words of encouragement and guidance. If you are not yet familiar with the habit of blessing, it may be a great starting point for your family.

Now, without further ado: Let's pray together, family!

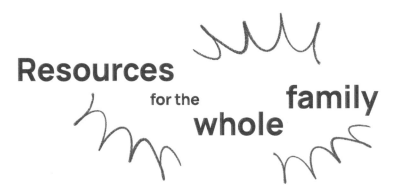

Resources for the whole family

21 Days is for adults + teens, too!

If you don't have a copy of the 21 Days of Prayer + Fasting 2025 book for adults and teens, which includes a section for notes, download a copy from **FoursquarePrayer.org** or buy one on Amazon.

Prayer + fasting resources

Looking for resources on prayer and fasting, or even how to talk about the Holy Spirit with the youngest members of your church and family? Visit **Foursquare.Church/21DOP-kids-resources** and you'll find companion books, blogs and podcasts that include:
- Practical prayer resources for kids +parents
- How the Holy Spirit helps us pray
- Creative ideas for family prayer time
- Why and how to engage in prayers of blessing

Church leaders + NextGen pastors

You are free to reproduce this Family Moments guide for your church or ministry, but it should be distributed at no cost. Visit **FoursquarePrayer.org** to sign up for daily email reminders and to find helpful resources as you communicate and gather as a family around prayer.

También disponible en español

Visite **OracionCuadrangular.org** y descargue o compre el libro completo de 21 Días de Ayuno + Oración 2025, así como el libro Momentos en Familia para sus hijos. También encontrará recursos para ayunar y orar, así como el kit de recursos de la iglesia de este año, para que toda su iglesia pueda comenzar el año orando juntos. Encuentre todo lo que necesita en **OracionCuadrangular.org**

Get ready for all 21 days

Ready to jump into Family Moments with your family? The following list of supplies will be needed in order to complete the daily activities during 21 Days of Prayer + Fasting. We can't wait to hear how families are praying together!

- Drawing supplies (paper, markers etc.)
- 3 tarnished pennies
- 3 small cups, each with one experiment solution:
  - **Cup 1:** 2 tbsp vinegar mixed with 1 tsp salt
  - **Cup 2:** 2 tbsp ketchup
  - **Cup 3:** 2 tbsp lemon juice mixed with 1 tsp salt
- A flashlight without batteries
- Batteries for the flashlight
- Marbles, Lego bricks or other non-metal small objects
- Vitamin C chewable tablet (or a spoonful of sugar)
- Blindfold
- Candy or other treats
- A variety of coins
- Aluminum foil
- Magnifying glass (optional)
- Backpack
- Large books or other heavy objects
- Sticky notes
- Gift bag
- Paper for drawing or a printed photo of each family member
- Print this spiritual gifts infographic: **Foursquare.Church/SpiritualGifts-FM2025**
- Clear jar or small box
- Small squares of paper
- Thank-you cards
- A deep plate or shallow, wide bowl
- Pepper
- Liquid dish soap
- A family-friendly jigsaw puzzle
- 2 oranges
- Print this world map: **Foursquare.Church/Map-FM2025**

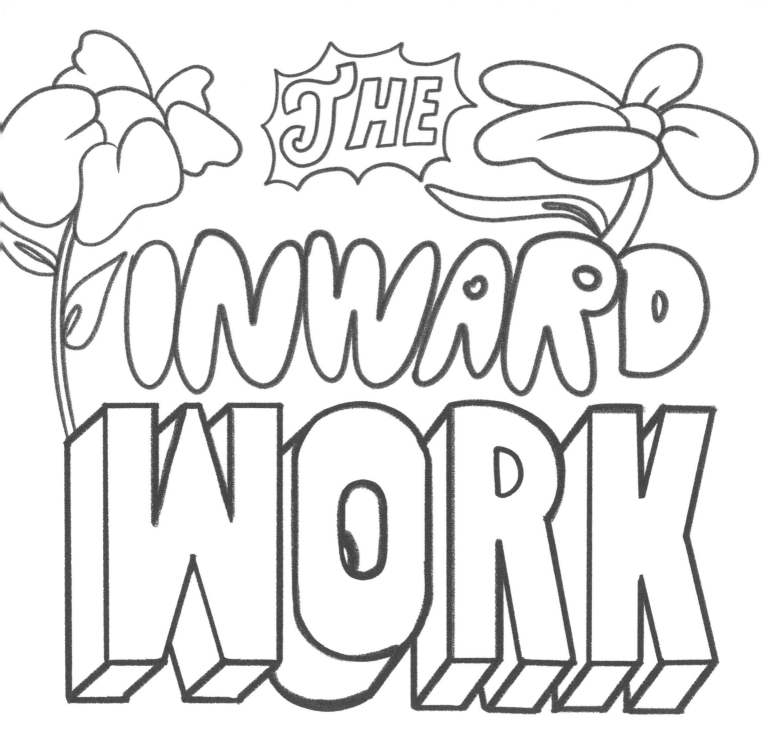

THE INWARD WORK

When we choose to follow Jesus and confess Him as our Savior, God promises us the gift of the Holy Spirit. Who is the Holy Spirit? The Holy Spirit is fully God, part of the Trinity. The Bible tells us that the Holy Spirit guides us, helps us with temptation, empowers us to live as new creations and reminds us that we are God's children. Let's discover more about the Holy Spirit together!

A 21-Day activity

Throughout the book, we'll invite you to write down each theme's sentence, given below, on a half or full sheet of paper. Feel free to be as simple or elaborate in your lettering and coloring as you like. On day 21, your family will have the opportunity to do something with the seven paper segments to celebrate completing your prayer journey.

ON THE SPIRIT

Here's the first sentence:
I pray that God will use His glorious riches to make you strong. May His Holy Spirit give you His power deep down inside you.

Day 01

RENEWED by the **Spirit**

God makes all things new, including you and me!

Today's Scripture

"He saved us, not because of righteous things we had done, but because of his mercy. He saved us through the washing of rebirth and renewal by the Holy Spirit, whom he poured out on us generously through Jesus Christ our Savior."

—Titus 3:5-6 (NIV)

Supplies

- 3 tarnished pennies
- 3 small cups, each with one experiment solution:
  Cup 1: 2 tbsp vinegar mixed with 1 tsp salt
  Cup 2: 2 tbsp ketchup
  Cup 3: 2 tbsp lemon juice mixed with 1 tsp salt
- A fourth cup filled with water

Reflect on the Word

When God's Holy Spirit works in us, He removes our sin and renews us—makes us new. Let's do a science experiment and discover how something tarnished can be renewed.

Place one penny in each cup; cover the pennies with each solution. As you wait five minutes for the solutions to work, take guesses on which cups will best clean the coins. After five minutes, take out the pennies one at a time. Rinse them in the cup of water and place them on a paper towel. Compare the coins and make a conclusion about which solution best renewed the tarnished coin.

In today's verse, we read that sin had once separated us from God, but Jesus' death and resurrection healed this relationship. When we choose to follow Jesus, we are made new by God's power—renewed by the Holy Spirit! Consider sharing with your children a way God's Spirit has renewed you.

**Reflect,
pray + bless**

01 ———— Reflect: As a follower of Jesus, you don't have to try to become a new creation. You just are one! When you stay connected to God, the Holy Spirit will renew you and grow new life in you.

02 ———— Pray: Give each family member the opportunity to hold the renewed coin. Invite the person holding the coin to complete the following prayer: "God, thank you for_____ . Please help me with _____."

03 ———— Bless: "[Child's name], may God's Spirit renew you, making you more like Him."

Notes & DRAWINGS

YOUR DRAWINGS HERE →

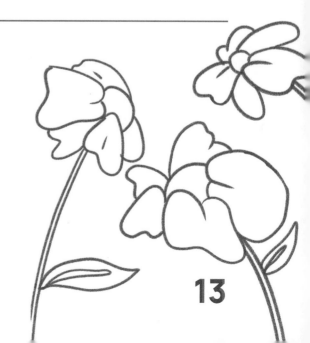

Day 02

Made alive in Christ

God's Spirit gives us power to live for Jesus.

Today's Scripture

"The Spirit of the God who raised Jesus from the dead is living in you. So the God who raised Christ from the dead will also give life to your bodies. He will do this because of his Spirit who lives in you."
—Romans 8:11 (NIRV)

Additional Scripture

1 Corinthians 6:19

Supplies

- A flashlight without batteries
- Batteries for the flashlight
- Marbles, Lego bricks or other non-metal small objects

Reflect on the Word

Parents or church leaders should darken the room and invite someone to try to turn on the flashlight without batteries. When it doesn't come on, help them discover why the flashlight isn't working. Try problem solving by putting marbles in the flashlight. Act confident that these will fix it. Does the flashlight work? Continue with other small objects for a while. Finally, insert the batteries.

Just like the flashlight had to be filled with the right energy, the batteries, we need to be filled with the Holy Spirit to be all God designed for us to be. God created us to be a home for His Holy Spirit. What happened when we tried to make the flashlight work using other things?

Sometimes people try using the wrong things to make their lives work. What are some of those things? When we choose to trust and follow Jesus, we have God's Spirit living in us (1 Cor. 6:19), giving us the power to live for Jesus like we were created to.

**Reflect,
pray + bless**

01 ——— Reflect: God created us to be a home for His Holy Spirit. When we choose to trust and follow Jesus, the Holy Spirit lives in us, helping us become all God created us to be.

02 ——— Pray: Darken the room and turn on the flashlight. Sit together and invite each family member to wonder about the awesome Holy Spirit power that raised Jesus from the dead. Tell a Holy Ghost story! Take turns thanking God that He created us to be homes for that very same Spirit through Jesus' death and resurrection.

03 ——— Bless: "[Child's name], may you become a home for the Holy Spirit through trusting and following Jesus, becoming all God has created you to be."

Notes

YOUR DRAWINGS HERE →

Day 03   Beloved  of God

God is more than a ruler or creator—He's there for us as our heavenly Dad, too.

Today's Scripture

"And because we are his children, God has sent the Spirit of his Son into our hearts, prompting us to call out, 'Abba, Father.' Now you are no longer a slave but God's own child. And since you are his child, God has made you his heir."

—Galatians 4:6-7 (NLT)

Supplies

- Paper
- Coloring supplies (markers, crayons, etc.)
- "Who You Say I Am" song by Yancy (link below)

Reflect on the Word

What are words you would use to describe yourself? Share with one another.

What are the words God uses to describe us? Some examples from the Bible include loved, chosen, redeemed, known, forgiven, beloved and adopted.

Distribute the paper and coloring supplies. Take time to quietly pray and respond to the question, "God, who do You say that I am?" Play the song while family members illustrate words or pictures that come to mind. At the end of the song, take time to share your drawings and pray together.

Digital resource

Listen to the song from Yancy at **Foursquare.Church/Yancy**

**Reflect,
pray + bless**

01 ——— Reflect: Do you know God loves you and calls you His child?

02 ——— Pray: We never have to be afraid when we come before God because we are children of the King. But we can still approach Him as King, with reverence. Try praying together in a bowed posture, as one might in front of a king.

03 ——— Bless: "[Child's name], may you know that your heavenly Father loves you. May you see yourself reflected in the eyes of the Father. You are a gift, you are beloved, you have been chosen, and you are a child of God."

Notes  DRAWINGS

_____

_____

_____

YOUR
DRAWINGS
HERE

LIFE IN

A promise for all believers is that God's presence dwells inside them. The power of God is not limited by age, time spent following Him or education level. The promise of His Spirit to comfort, teach, guide and empower for His glory is available to you! May you prayerfully step into the next three days, surrendering to the work of the Spirit with eyes open to see Him on display.

18

A 21-Day activity
Write out part two of your prayer
journey on a piece of paper.
Feel free to make it fancy!

Remember that Christ lives in your
heart because you believe in Him.

THE

SPIRIT

Day 04 Praise and thanksgiving

In every part of our life, in each moment of our day, we can find things to thank God for!

Today's Scripture

"Rejoice always, pray continually, give thanks in all circumstances; for this is God's will for you in Christ Jesus."
—1 Thessalonians 5:16-18 (NIV)

Reflect on the Word

We were made to worship God. Worship starts by simply thinking about Him—who He is, what He has done, what He is doing. Even when things are hard or we don't feel like it, the Holy Spirit helps us worship. Praise and thanksgiving are important ways we worship God. When we praise God, we focus on who He is. When we thank God, we're thanking Him for what He has done.

Put this thankful attitude to work with a family scavenger hunt. For the first round, everyone finds something they're thankful for. Items can be symbolic; for example, a water bottle might remind you to thank God for clean water. Gather items and share your responses.

For the second round, everyone finds something that describes God (a praise item). For example, a toy animal might remind you to praise God as Creator, or a bandage might remind you that God heals. Once again, share your responses with one another, and be encouraging.

**Reflect,
pray + bless**

01 ——— Reflect: What could it look like to give God thanks and praise in your daily routine?

02 ——— Pray: Using the letters of your last name, craft a family prayer of praise and thanksgiving. For each letter, share a word of praise or something you're thankful for that begins with that letter, or includes it, if that's easier for little ones.

03 ——— Bless: "[Child's name], give thanks to the Lord, for He is good! His faithful love endures forever. May you always remember that you are loved and that you were made to worship God."

Notes

_____

_____

_____

YOUR DRAWINGS HERE →

Day 05  Repentance and  forgiveness

All of us have sinned and are in need of God's forgiveness.

Today's Scripture

"Nevertheless I tell you the truth. It is to your advantage that I go away; for if I do not go away, the Helper will not come to you; but if I depart, I will send Him to you. And when He has come, He will convict the world of sin, and of righteousness, and of judgment: of sin, because they do not believe in Me; of righteousness, because I go to My Father and you see Me no more; of judgment, because the ruler of this world is judged."
—John 16:7-11 (NKJV)

Additional Scripture

Luke 15:11-32

Supplies

- Vitamin C chewable tablet (or a spoonful of sugar)
- Clear glass of warm water

Reflect on the Word

Read the story of the prodigal son found in Luke 15:11-32 (using a storybook Bible if needed for little ones). Bonus points for acting out the parable as you read!

Why do you think Jesus told this story? What do we learn about God from the story? The Bible tells us we all sin. We all do things our way instead of God's way sometimes. So, the question becomes, what do we do when we sin?

God invites us to repent and experience His promised forgiveness. To repent means to turn away from sin and turn toward God. When we confess our sins to God, we are promised forgiveness because of the sacrifice of Jesus.

Parents, now is a great time to share an example of when the Holy Spirit prompted you to repent, and you experienced God's forgiveness.

**Reflect,
pray + bless**

01 ———— Reflect: Remind children that "God is faithful and fair. If we confess our sins, he will forgive our sins. He will forgive every wrong thing we have done. He will make us pure" (1 John 1:9, NIRV).

02 ———— Pray: Ask God, "Is there any sin in my life I need to confess?" As you talk to God, add the tablet to the water and watch it dissolve. Let it remind you of God's promised forgiveness and the wiping away of our sins.

03 ———— Bless: "[Child's name], may you always know that God loves you. In the moments when you stumble, may you always return to Him, experience His forgiveness and be made pure again."

Notes + DRAWINGS

_____

_____

_____

YOUR DRAWINGS HERE

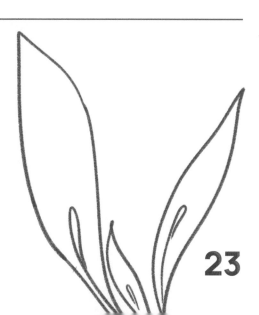

Day 06

Finding our way through life can be challenging, but we have a Helper to guide us, the Holy Spirit.

Today's Scripture

"However, when He, the Spirit of truth, has come, He will guide you into all truth ..."
—John 16:13 (NKJV)

Additional Scripture

John 14:15-17

Supplies

- Blindfold
- Candy or other treats

Reflect on the Word

Parents: Before starting, hide treats around the house.

It can be challenging to know what is true and right. Have you ever thought, "It would be easier to follow Jesus if He was still living as a human?" Right before His death and resurrection, Jesus told his friends that He would be leaving them. They became anxious, wondering, "What will we do? Who will we follow?" Read John 14:15-17.

Who is the Helper? What did Jesus promise the Helper would do?

Take turns navigating blindfolded through the house, guided by a family member's voice, to find a hidden treat. Invite other family members to call out wrong directions. Take turns, navigating to different rooms.

Enjoy your treats as you talk and pray together. Was it easy to hear the correct guiding voice? How is this like listening to the Holy Spirit? What "voices" in our lives might keep us from listening to the Holy Spirit?

**Reflect,
pray + bless**

01 ——— Reflect: When we listen, the Holy Spirit helps us know what to do.

02 ——— Pray: Invite everyone to share stories about when they experienced Holy Spirit guidance to know what to do. Pray, thanking God for the gift of the Holy Spirit's guidance.

03 ——— Bless: "[Child's name], may you have ears to hear and a heart that desires to listen for the Holy Spirit's guidance in your life. As you listen, may you experience His blessing of walking in what is right and true."

Notes

_____

_____

_____

YOUR DRAWINGS HERE

THE TRANSFORMING TRAINING

What is God's plan for us? That we would become more like Jesus (see 2 Cor. 3:18). And how do we become more like Him? We abide, we rest in God's presence, and we spend time with Him. The Bible makes it clear that the Holy Spirit is God's power at work in us. He is responsible for transformation. Set aside time to rest and be in His presence with eyes open to see the power of God at work in the days ahead.

A 21-Day activity
Keep on writing and decorating those sentences. We're already one-third of the way done with our 21-day journey! Here's part three to record on a half or full sheet of paper:

And I pray that your love will have deep roots. I pray that it will have a strong foundation.

Day 07

SPIRIT-sourced **transformation**

God can change and transform us into His image through His Holy Spirit and the ministry of other believers, if we allow it.

Today's Scripture

"... And the Lord—who is the Spirit—makes us more and more like Him as we are changed into His glorious image."
—2 Corinthians 3:18 (NLT)

Additional Scripture

Acts 3:1-10

Supplies

- A variety of coins
- Aluminum foil
- Markers
- Paper
- Optional: magnifying glass

Reflect on the Word

Spread out the coins on a table and examine them together. Use the magnifying glass if you have one. Talk about the differences you see. Now invite family members to lay a piece of aluminum foil flat on top of a coin. Using the long edge of the marker like a rolling pin, rub across the foil over the coin, creating an impression on the foil. Do this with other coins as interest allows.

How was the aluminum foil changed? God is like the coin, and we are like the foil. Talk about how the foil now reflects the image of the coin.

Read today's verse, 2 Cor. 3:18. The Holy Spirit has the power to transform us. The story of Peter provides a powerful example. When Peter was baptized with the Holy Spirit, he was transformed from a fearful, stubborn denier of Jesus into a bold, courageous preacher who performed miracles in Jesus' name (see Acts 2). Then he was able to transform others, with God's help.

Read Acts 3:1-10 together to learn how he helped transform someone.

Reflect, pray + bless

01 —————— Reflect: The Holy Spirit has the power to transform me to make me more like Jesus.

02 —————— Pray: Invite each family member to draw a picture of themselves. Write a word or words around the picture in response to this question: "In what ways do you want the Holy Spirit to transform you to reflect the image of Jesus?" Pray for these things.

03 —————— Bless: "[Child's name], may you invite the Holy Spirit to continue to shape you into the image of Jesus, bringing the light and hope of His love to all you encounter."

Notes & DRAWINGS

YOUR DRAWINGS HERE

Day 08 — Spirit-governed thoughts

What do you do when you have negative or sinful thoughts?
How does God help us overcome that kind of thinking?

Today's Scripture

"Those who are dominated by the sinful nature think about sinful things, but those who are controlled by the Holy Spirit think about things that please the Spirit. So letting your sinful nature control your mind leads to death. But letting the Spirit control your mind leads to life and peace."
—Romans 8:5-6 (NLT)

Reflect on the Word

Our days are filled with thoughts, some positive, some negative, many random. An incredible truth about following Jesus and being filled with the Holy Spirit is that God speaks to us even through our own thoughts! He can give us a mind set on Him and His truth.

Now, that doesn't mean the negative, angry, unkind thoughts totally go away. So, what do we do in those moments?

We can't outthink negative thoughts in our own strength, but we can certainly ask for God's help. One way to set your mind on the Spirit is to speak God's truth over your thoughts.

Pick a family Bible verse (for example, Ps. 136:1, Eph. 4:32, Phil. 4:8, or find your own). Write down the verse and memorize it by turning it into a song or pairing it with motions.

Reflect, pray + bless

01 ———— Reflect: "The thoughts of a person ruled by sin bring death. But the mind ruled by the Spirit brings life and peace." Rom. 8:6 (NIRV)

02 ———— Pray: In the center of a piece of paper, write "God" and circle it. From there, draw lines branching out and write down or doodle/draw things you pray for. If needed, add more branches off these as related needs arise (e.g., God – School Safety – My Teachers). Ask God to direct your prayers and doodle what comes to mind.

03 ———— Bless: "[Child's name], 'whatever is true, whatever is honorable, whatever is right, whatever is pure, whatever is lovely, whatever is admirable—if anything is excellent or praiseworthy—think on these things. And the God of peace will be with you.'" Phil. 4:8-9 (NIV)

Notes + DRAWINGS

YOUR DRAWINGS HERE

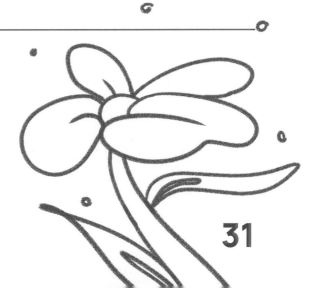

Day 09

Spirit-formed character and creativity

What does it mean to "bear fruit" in our lives, and how do we honor God doing that?

Today's Scripture

"But the fruit of the Spirit is love, joy, peace, patience, kindness, goodness, faithfulness, gentleness, self-control; against such things there is no law."
—Galatians 5:22-23 (ESV)

Additional Scripture

John 15:7-8

Supplies

- Markers or crayons
- Paper

Reflect on the Word

What's your favorite fruit? How does it grow to become the fruit you like so much? Jesus taught that just like you can identify a tree by its fruit, you can identify people by their actions—by what they do and say (Matt. 7:15-20).

No apple ever said, "I'm going to try really, really hard to become an apple!" Apples (as well as other fruit) just pop out when the tree gets what it needs: good soil, water and sunshine.

As followers of Jesus, when we take time to simply be with Jesus by praying, reading His Word and listening to Him, we get what we need for the Holy Spirit to work a miracle through us. The Holy Spirit changes us to be more and more like Jesus, and people will see and experience the fruit of His Spirit popping out of our lives!

Digital resource

Check out this video from National Geographic about an amazing tree that grows 40 kinds of fruit: **Foursquare.Church/FruitVideo**

**Reflect,
pray + bless**

01 ———— Reflect: As we spend time with Jesus, the Holy Spirit changes us, making us more and more like Jesus.

02 ———— Pray: On a piece of paper, write down the fruits of the Spirit, and if you like, draw a different fruit to symbolize each. Which of the fruits of the Spirit do you observe in different family members? Name these to one another, then pray together, thanking God for the Spirit's transforming work in your family.

03 ———— Bless: "[Child's name], may you desire to spend time with Jesus, making way for the Holy Spirit to work in you. And may your life reflect the fruit of His Spirit as He makes you more and more like Jesus."

Notes

_____

_____

_____

YOUR
DRAWINGS
HERE

Picture this: You've been told that tomorrow, you get to go on an adventure! You're filled with anticipation and excitement, imagining what's to come. Walking as a Holy-Spirit-powered follower of Jesus can make your life an adventure every day. From the moment you wake, the Holy Spirit invites you to experience your day listening and responding to Him, whether by yourself or interacting with others. The adventure comes in noticing and responding, allowing the Holy Spirit to work through you to bless others.

THE Manifestation

A 21-Day activity
As you prepare for the next few days, here's part four to write and set aside:

May you have power together with all the Lord's holy people to understand Christ's love.

OF THE SPIRIT

35

Day 10 Praying in the SPIRIT

When we don't know how to pray, the Holy Spirit is an intercessor who prays on our behalf.

Today's Scripture

"And the Holy Spirit helps us in our weakness. For example, we don't know what God wants us to pray for. But the Holy Spirit prays for us with groanings that cannot be expressed in words. And the Father who knows all hearts knows what the Spirit is saying, for the Spirit pleads for us believers in harmony with God's own will."

—Romans 8:26-27 (NLT)

Supplies

- Backpack
- Large books or other heavy objects
- Sticky notes

Reflect on the Word

First, label some sticky notes with negative emotions like fear, worry, anger, sadness, loneliness or doubt. Have kids place a sticky note of their choosing on one of the heavy books, until each heavy item is labeled. Then fill a backpack with the heavy items and let your children try carrying it around. Could they wear this all day? Why not?

Sometimes we're so afraid or worried about something, we don't even know how to pray about it. It feels like a heavy burden.

In today's verses, we discover that the Holy Spirit prays for us, having all the right words even when we don't have any. The Spirit is an intercessor, or someone who prays our prayers for us.

Read the passage again. Transfer the backpack from the child to an adult, and walk around together. Removing the heavy backpack reminds us how the Holy Spirit takes our troubles and brings them before God. He walks beside us, carrying the weight.

**Reflect,
pray + bless**

01 ——— Reflect: The Holy Spirit takes our burdens, praying our prayers for us, having all the right words when we don't have any.

02 ——— Pray: Remove the objects from the backpack, using the labels as prompts for sharing burdens to bring before the Holy Spirit. After sharing, sit quietly with open hands, symbolizing releasing your burdens to the Holy Spirit. Close in prayer by thanking God for the gift of His Holy Spirit.

03 ——— Bless: "[Child's name], may you remember to rely on the Holy Spirit to lift your burdens, trusting Him to pray on your behalf when you don't have the words."

Notes + DRAWINGS

_____

_____

_____

YOUR
DRAWINGS
HERE

Day 11

Spiritual gifts

There are many gifts of the Holy Spirit, and only God decides how each person is uniquely gifted for ministry.

Today's Scripture

"There are different kinds of spiritual gifts, but the same Spirit is the source of them all. There are different kinds of service, but we serve the same Lord. God works in different ways, but it is the same God who does the work in all of us. A spiritual gift is given to each of us so we can help each other."

—1 Corinthians 12: 4-7 (NLT)

Supplies

- Gift bag
- Paper for drawing or a printed photo of each family member
- Markers

Reflect on the Word

Show the gift bag. Ask, "What do you think when you see a gift bag?" Share with one another some of your all-time favorite gifts you've received.

Did you know the Holy Spirit also gives gifts? Unlike the favorites you shared, we can't pull Holy Spirit gifts out of a bag. These gifts are special abilities that help us grow closer to Jesus and allow us to play our part in God's big story. It's never too early to look for hints of the Holy Spirit's gifts in you.

Have each family member draw a self-portrait, or use printed photos. One person at a time, call out the strengths you observe in one another, while writing these words around the self-portraits or photos. Could any of these strengths point to spiritual gifts in one another?

Digital resource

God's gift: Learn more about spiritual gifts with this infographic!
Foursquare.Church/SpiritualGifts-FM2025

Reflect, pray + bless

01 ——— Reflect: The Holy Spirit gives spiritual gifts to followers of Jesus, equipping them to live their part in God's big story.

02 ——— Pray: Use a "prayer chair." Invite a family member to sit in the designated chair. Invite all other family members to gather around to pray, naming the strengths written on their photo or self-portrait to contend for an unfolding revelation and embracing of that person's spiritual gifts. Repeat with all other family members.

03 ——— Bless: "[Child's name], we celebrate the gifts the Holy Spirit has placed in you. May these gifts be nurtured to maturity, empowering you to bless others, living out your part in God's big story."

Notes  DRAWINGS

YOUR DRAWINGS HERE →

Day 12  Miracles

On a daily basis, God is at work all around us, doing the impossible in big and small ways; we just need to take notice of Him.

Today's Scripture

"And God confirmed the message by giving signs and wonders and various miracles and gifts of the Holy Spirit whenever he chose."
—Hebrews 2:4 (NLT)

Supplies

- Clear jar or small box
- Markers
- Squares of paper

Reflect on the Word

What comes to mind when you hear the word "miracles"? Miracles come in big and small moments. Sometimes miracles are super obvious, and other times they're more private. The Bible reveals that a miracle is an act of God, a time when God shows up and gets the glory.

Does God still do miracles today? Yes! He continues to answer prayers, to heal and to provide.

Consider the greatest miracle we can experience: becoming a Christian. By faith in Jesus, who miraculously rose from the dead, God does the impossible and transforms us into new creations.

What is a miracle you've experienced or witnessed? Share stories. Next, consider starting a family "miracle box." Whenever you witness a miracle, answer to prayer or "God sighting," write or draw it on a piece of paper and place it in the box or jar. When the jar is full, or at the end of a month or year, pull them out and read them together to reflect.

May we always be people who notice God's work and share His miracles with others!

Reflect, pray + bless

01 —— Reflect: God works miracles. Reflect on a miracle from Scripture, one from your own life or one that you've witnessed.

02 —— Pray: If weather allows, go outside and look at the stars. Soak in God's grandness as you share your prayers with Him.

03 —— Bless: "[Child's name], may you put your trust in our miracle-working God. May you have faith to pray the big prayers and eyes to see God on display."

Notes

YOUR DRAWINGS HERE

The church, the body of Christ, is people who follow Jesus. We're the church on Sunday morning when we gather together. We're also the church when we help a neighbor or care for a friend. Any time that we live as Jesus would out in the world, we are being the church. We are displaying the life and love of God to the people around us! Enjoy discovering what it means to be the church: people whom God equips and empowers to be courageous and unified, reflecting His love and power to a hurting world.

A 21-Day activity
As you prepare for the theme of the next three days, here's part five to write down on a full or half sheet of paper:

May you know how wide and long and high and deep it is.

43

Day 13

A spiritual church

The Bible says we are the church. But, what does that mean?

Today's Scripture

"You also, like living stones, are being built into a spiritual house to be a holy priesthood, offering spiritual sacrifices acceptable to God through Jesus Christ."
—1 Peter 2:5 (NIV)

Additional Scripture

Acts 2:41-47

Supplies

- Thank-you cards
- Pens

Reflect on the Word

You are the church! The church is so much more than a building or service—the church is people who follow Jesus. That means wherever we go, the church goes! In the Old Testament, God's Spirit dwelled with His people in the temple. But when Jesus paid the price for our sins, God poured out His Spirit for all believers, anywhere they are. That Spirit now lives in us. We are carriers of the presence of God.

Read Acts 2:41-47. Encourage everyone to pay close attention to new ways to describe the church. After reading, share what you learned about the church.

How is the church in Acts 2 similar to the church today? How is it different? One of the ways we can operate as God's church is to provide encouragement and prayer to our own local church community. Consider writing a thank-you card or blessing note to a volunteer, pastor, peer or another family from your church.

Digital resource

What is the church? After reading the story in Acts 2, check out the video from LifeKids! **Foursquare.Church/21DOP-Acts2**

Reflect, pray + bless

01 ——— Reflect: God's presence dwells in His children. We are the church!

02 ——— Pray: Ask God who to pray for in your faith community. As a family, pray out loud for specific people that come to mind.

03 ——— Bless: "[Child's name], may you always remember that wherever you go, God is with you and that He has chosen you to be the church."

Notes  DRAWINGS

YOUR DRAWINGS HERE →

Day 14

A **bold** and **courageous church**

Even the bravest person feels timid or fearful sometimes, but God can empower us to conquer those fears to share His love with the world.

Today's Scripture

"For the Spirit God gave us does not make us timid, but gives us power, love and self-discipline."

—2 Timothy 1:7 (NIV)

Supplies

- A deep plate or shallow, wide bowl
- Water
- Pepper
- Liquid dish soap

Reflect on the Word

Gather around the table and pour about 1 inch of water into the plate. Sprinkle a tablespoon of pepper on the water's surface. Ask: "Do you sometimes feel afraid to speak up as a follower of Jesus?" Allow family members to answer openly and honestly.

Sometimes our desire to be liked and accepted can overpower us, keeping us from doing what's right. Can you think of people in the Bible or from history who overcame fear to boldly show and tell others about Jesus? In today's verse, we're reminded that it is the Holy Spirit who gives this power, and it is available to us, too!

Invite a family member to dip their finger in the pepper water. What happens? Now, dip your finger into the dish soap and back into the water. What happens? How is the pepper moving away like the fear that flees when we trust the Holy Spirit to fill us with boldness and courage?

**Reflect,
pray + bless**

01 ———— Reflect: The Holy Spirit gives me the power to live boldly for Jesus, showing and telling others of His love and truth.

02 ———— Pray: Invite family members to share where they need to be filled with Holy Spirit boldness. Pray for each person, contending for the Holy Spirit to fill them with power, love and self-discipline.

03 ———— Bless: "[Child's name], like Timothy in the Bible, may you walk boldly, empowered by the Holy Spirit to show and tell those in your world of God's love and truth.

Notes

YOUR DRAWINGS HERE →

Day 15

A unified church

God's Spirit brings unity. It's only by His power that we can be unified as a family, church and community.

Today's Scripture

"As a prisoner for the Lord, then, I urge you to live a life worthy of the calling you have received. Be completely humble and gentle; be patient, bearing with one another in love. Make every effort to keep the unity of the Spirit through the bond of peace. There is one body and one Spirit, just as you were called to one hope when you were called; one Lord, one faith, one baptism; one God and Father of all, who is over all and through all and in all."

—Ephesians 4:1-6 (NIV)

Supplies

• A family-friendly jigsaw puzzle

Reflect on the Word

Gather around the table or sit on the floor and put the puzzle together as a team. What does it mean to be unified? Share responses and examples.

To be unified means to be brought together as one. Examine your puzzle. Each puzzle piece is different from all the others. It is one of a kind. Together with all the other pieces, it creates a unified picture. We're all different, uniquely created by God. And yet, even with our differences, the Holy Spirit still brings us together, like these puzzle pieces.

Without the Holy Spirit, it's impossible for us to be unified as believers. We all know loving others can be hard sometimes. The good news is that Jesus doesn't expect us to be able to love others on our own. The Holy Spirit helps us do that—He unifies believers!

**Reflect,
pray + bless**

01 ———— Reflect: "How good and pleasant it is when God's people live together in unity!" (Psalm 133:1, NIV).

02 ———— Pray: The Holy Spirit's power to unify is true for our world, our churches and our homes. Let's start in our homes. Pray over every family member with words of encouragement and truths about who God created them to be.

03 ———— Bless: "[Child's name], may you experience the unity God's Spirit brings. May you share God's love with others (even those who are hard to get along with), and may your life be marked by God's peace."

Notes DRAWINGS

_____

_____

_____

YOUR DRAWINGS HERE

DIRECTION

and

Life can be really confusing and challenging at times. And even when life is great, we still face important decisions that will affect our future. As Spirit-filled followers of Jesus, God has provided the Holy Spirit as our guide to navigate all of life. When we're not sure what's right or we're uncertain about a choice, we can rely on the Holy Spirit to help us. As we experience the blessing of responding to these prompts, our trust in the Holy Spirit as our good guide grows, and we experience all that God has for us. Isn't that amazing?

REVELATION

PROTECTION

A 21-Day activity

Oh, and remember to keep writing on a half or full sheet of paper. Here's your sixth sentence:

And may you know his love, even though it can't be known completely.

Day 16

Praying for guidance and direction

More than any person, law of the land or structure,
God is the most trustworthy being in the universe.

Today's Scripture

"Trust in the Lord with all your heart; do not depend on your own understanding. Seek His will in all you do, and He will show you which path to take."

—Proverbs 3:5-6 (NLT)

Supplies

- 9 sheets of paper
- Pen

Reflect on the Word

Write Proverbs 3:5-6 on several sheets of paper, dividing the verse out in 6-8 sections. Create a "path" with the papers on the floor. Travel the path, reciting the verse along the way. Mix things up by finding creative ways to travel the path (like jumping, skipping or crawling). What does it look like to trust in God? What does it mean to seek His will?

Trusting in God can be hard, but God is always trustworthy. When we say God is trustworthy, we mean that He is always good, He always loves us, He always hears us, and He always does what He says He'll do.

We can look in the Bible and read about God's trustworthiness. We can listen to other people share testimonies and hear that God is trustworthy. The Holy Spirit helps us trust Him more with the promise that He will show us which path to take.

**Reflect,
pray + bless**

01 ——— Reflect: We can trust God with our cares and fears, no matter how impossible or silly they may seem.

02 ——— Pray: Take a sheet of paper and draw a vertical line down the center to create two columns. Label the left column "Ways God has provided." Label the right column "Where I need to trust God." Prayerfully fill in both columns by writing or drawing pictures.

03 ——— Bless: "[Child's name], trust in God with all your heart; do not depend on your own understanding. May you seek Him in all you do, knowing that He will show you which path to take."

Notes & DRAWINGS

_____

_____

_____

YOUR DRAWINGS HERE →

Day 17 — Praying for covering and protection

The armor of God is not only a metaphor, but also protection in a very real spiritual battle for our souls.

Today's Scripture

"Finally, be strong in the Lord and in his mighty power. Put on the full armor of God, so that you can take your stand against the devil's schemes. For our struggle is not against flesh and blood, but against the rulers, against the authorities, against the powers of this dark world and against the spiritual forces of evil in the heavenly realms."

—Ephesians 6:10-12 (NIV)

Supplies

- 2 oranges
- Large bowl of water

Reflect on the Word

The world tells us the only real things are what we can physically see, but God tells us this isn't true. There is an unseen spiritual battle going on for our hearts and minds every day.

Read Ephesians 6:10–18 and encourage family members to close their eyes and visualize the different armor pieces. Also, family members can draw the different armor pieces as you read.

Being in a spiritual battle means we need a power that is not our own. God gives us what we need to stand up and fight in this real battle. As a final visual reminder of being equipped with the full armor of God, submerge two oranges in a water bowl (they should float). Remove the "armor" (peel) from one of the oranges and see what happens (the "armorless" orange will sink).

**Reflect,
pray + bless**

01 ——— Reflect: Prayer is a powerful and effective offensive weapon. It reminds us that God is already fully engaged in the battle and has already declared victory.

02 ——— Pray: What battles or fears are you facing right now? Share as a family. As a symbol of God's promised covering and protection, hold a blanket over each person as you pray God's power over the shared fears and battles.

03 ——— Bless: "[Child's name], may you be empowered to pray at all times and equipped with the armor of God to stand firm in any battle you face."

Notes + DRAWINGS

YOUR DRAWINGS HERE →

Day 18 Praying for discernment and revelation

The Holy Spirit is our best strategy for discovering and living in God's good plan for us.

Today's Scripture

"God has shown these things to us through His Spirit. The Spirit understands all things. He understands even the deep things of God. Who can know the thoughts of another person? Only a person's own spirit can know them. In the same way, only the Spirit of God knows God's thoughts. What we have received is not the spirit of the world. We have received the Spirit who is from God. The Spirit helps us understand what God has freely given us."

—1 Corinthians 2:10-12 (NIRV)

Reflect on the Word

Play 20 Questions together. One person thinks of a visible object in the house and writes it down. Everyone else asks yes-or-no questions to discover the object. Can you name the object in 20 questions? Continue to play as interest allows.

What was it like to figure out what people were thinking? Wonder outloud: is it hard to discover what God is thinking?

Sometimes we face big decisions, and it's hard to know what to do. Share a big decision you've made (e.g., moving, accepting a new job or picking a school). Whether it's a big decision or a smaller one, followers of Jesus seek God's wisdom. They know God loves them and wants them to live in His good plan. They trust Him to guide.

The good news? God has given the Holy Spirit, who helps us know what to do, no matter how big or small the decision might be.

**Reflect,
pray + bless**

01 ——— Reflect: The Holy Spirit helps us understand and know God's thoughts and plans, giving us direction to make wise decisions.

02 ——— Pray: Is there an area of your life where you need God's wisdom? Share and write responses down. Choose one situation and pray, asking the Holy Spirit for discernment and taking time to listen. When done, share anything you feel the Holy Spirit revealed.

03 ——— Bless: "[Child's name], may you always remember that God loves you, knows you and desires for you to live in His good plan. May you quickly seek the Holy Spirit for wisdom and discernment to live in that good plan."

Notes

_____

_____

_____

YOUR
DRAWINGS
HERE

58

Jesus is the Good News, and He invites us to follow Him and be His disciples. That's our job: to be His disciples and to make disciples, according to Matt. 28. He didn't expect us to do it on our own, so He gave us the gift of the Holy Spirit. We do not have the power to transform hearts and lives—that's His job. We're invited to follow, letting Him direct our steps and giving us what we need as His disciples. Consider speaking this simple prayer as a family as you prepare for the final three days of 21 Days of Prayer + Fasting: "God, where You lead us, we will go."

A 21-Day activity
Here's your final sentence to write! After writing out the final message, you should have seven sheets of paper with the different parts. You'll have the opportunity to gather all the papers on day 21 and assemble the message!

Then you will be filled with everything God has for you.

Day 19  Power to be witnesses for Jesus

Jesus told us to go and make disciples of all nations, but where and how can we share the love of God ourselves?

Today's Scripture

"But you shall receive power when the Holy Spirit has come upon you; and you shall be witnesses to Me in Jerusalem, and in all Judea and Samaria, and to the end of the earth."

—Acts 1:8 (NKJV)

Supplies

- Print this world map: **Foursquare.Church/Map-FM2025**

Reflect on the Word

Read the story of Pentecost in Acts 1:4-11 and Acts 2, or read it in a storybook Bible. How did you see the Holy Spirit at work in the story? What does it mean to be a witness?

To be a witness for Jesus means that we share the truth that we have experienced and heard. God takes care of the heart transformation.

Take out your map of the world, and point out any places familiar to your family. For the disciples, Jerusalem was their city, Judea was kind of like their state, and we can translate Samaria as their country.

On your map, locate and draw a circle around your own city using a pencil or your finger. Next, draw circles around your state and then your country. Discuss what it might look like to be a witness for Jesus in each of those regions.

**Reflect,
pray + bless**

01 ———— Reflect: You were made in God's image to reflect Him to the world. By the power of the Holy Spirit, your life bears witness to God's love, character and truth.

02 ———— Pray: In each circle of the map (city, state, country, entire world), write the name of a person or place you're praying for. Pray as a family and display the map in your home as a prayer reminder.

03 ———— Bless: "[Child's name], may you be filled with power from God's Spirit to know His great love and to be His witness in [name of your city] and in all [name of your state] and [name of your country], and to the ends of the earth."

Notes + DRAWINGS

_____

_____

_____

YOUR DRAWINGS HERE →

Day 20 Power to preach and demonstrate the gospel

A prayer walk while wearing the armor of God is a wonderful way to begin to be a witness for Jesus.

Today's Scripture

"A final word: Be strong in the Lord and in his mighty power. Put on all of God's armor so that you will be able to stand firm against all strategies of the devil. ... For shoes, put on the peace that comes from the Good News so that you will be fully prepared.

—Ephesians 6:10-11,15 (NLT)

Reflect on the Word

Invite family members to share which pair of shoes is their favorite. Why are they your favorites?

In Ephesians 6, we are encouraged to put on God's armor, and in place of shoes is "the peace that comes from the Good News" (v.15). Those shoes seem different than any of our favorites. Do you think they're more powerful? More protective?

The Holy Spirit gives us power to walk in His peace, taking the message of Jesus' love and forgiveness wherever we go. Every day brings opportunities to show and tell others of His love.

Go on a family prayer walk (See ideas in the prayer section below). Beyond today, build this prayerful mindset into your family's culture by noting and acting upon prayer opportunities within your daily rhythms (e.g., grocery shopping, at the park, at activities or eating at restaurants).

**Reflect,
pray + bless**

01 ———— Reflect: The Holy Spirit is at work all around me, wherever I go. When I'm watchful, I'll discover exciting opportunities to pray for others, showing and telling the Good News of Jesus.

02 ———— Pray: Go on a family prayer walk at a location of your choosing (e.g., your neighborhood, the mall or a park). While walking, be watchful for opportunities to pray for needs you see or sense, praying in the moment, or note the needs and pray when you return home.

03 ———— Bless: "[Child's name], may you approach each day, powered by the Holy Spirit, and watchful for opportunities to pray, bringing the Good News of Jesus into the situations you encounter."

Notes

_____

_____

_____

YOUR DRAWINGS HERE →

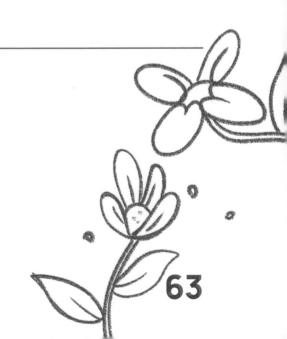

Day 21   Power to live in the fullness of God's love

Thanks be to God for the blessings He gives us, but especially for the gift of His Holy Spirit to guide us.

Today's Scripture

"I pray that He will use His glorious riches to make you strong. May His Holy Spirit give you His power deep down inside you. Then Christ will live in your hearts because you believe in Him. And I pray that your love will have deep roots. I pray that it will have a strong foundation. May you have power together with all the Lord's holy people to understand Christ's love. May you know how wide and long and high and deep it is. And may you know His love, even though it can't be known completely. Then you will be filled with everything God has for you."
—Ephesians 3:16-19 (NIRV)

Reflect on the Word

Congratulations! You have explored Scripture and prayed together faithfully for 21 days, experiencing the Holy Spirit in so many dimensions. Let's remember and celebrate this journey.

What were your favorite activities? What new discoveries did you make about the Holy Spirit? How have you seen the Holy Spirit working through your prayers? Record these to use as prayer prompts.

You were invited to write some sentences throughout this journey. Retrieve those and work together to assemble them, using Today's Scripture (above) as your guide. Once assembled, read this powerful blessing together.

What is the power that allows us to know and experience all the love God intends for us? You might consider gluing the assembled verse to a piece of construction paper or posterboard and posting it in your home as a reminder to pray this blessing over your family as the Holy Spirit leads.

**Reflect,
pray + bless**

01 ———— Reflect: The Holy Spirit is God's amazing gift to us, giving us the power to live in Jesus' immense love, paving the way for us to accomplish all the kingdom work He has planned for us.

02 ———— Pray: Thank God for ways the Holy Spirit empowered you that stand out from your prayer journey. Use the prayer prompts from your conversation to guide your prayers of thankfulness.

03 ———— Bless: Conclude by praying Eph. 3:16-19 as a blessing over each family member.

Notes + DRAWINGS

_____

_____

_____

YOUR DRAWINGS HERE →

A word of thanks

Thank you for joining us for 21 Days of Prayer + Fasting 2025. Our greatest desire is that you grew as a family, united on mission and learned from one another, as well. A special thanks goes out to everyone who worked on and prayed over this devotional. We hope the last 21 days have been a blessing and that your family will continue together in prayer and fellowship.

The 21 Days of Prayer + Fasting 2025 Team

Editors
Marcia Graham
Amanda Borowski
Bill Shepson

Content + Project Coordination
Erin Edquist
Jordan McKenna
Ashleigh Rich

Spanish Translation + Coordination
Diana Edwards
Raul Irigoyen
Rebekka Otremba
Melisa Prieto

Design, Photography + Illustrations
Josh Hernandez
PJ Moon

Website
Ben Gurrad

Video
Caique Morais

Social Media
Luke La Vine

Special thanks to our writers + contributors:
Daniel A. Brown, Ph.D.; Molly DuQue; John Fehlen;
Timmy Hensel; Melinda Kinsman; Heidi Messner;
Randy Remington; Steve Schell; Jerry Stott, Ph.D.;
Nakisha Wenzel; Andrew Williams, Ph.D.; Lindsay Willis

"And pray in the Spirit on all occasions with all kinds of prayers and requests. With this in mind, be alert and always keep on praying for all the Lord's people" (Eph. 6:18, NIV).

The Foursquare Church is kicking off January 2025 with a time of intentional prayer together. And your littlest pray-ers are welcome to join, too!

This Family Moments edition of **21 Days of Prayer + Fasting 2025** offers daily Scripture, fun activities and intentional times of prayer, all with your preschool and elementary-aged child in mind.

Join the global Foursquare community in Spirit-filled prayer Jan. 6-26, 2025, and get ready for God to move in mighty ways.

Find additional resources, including the **21 Days of Prayer + Fasting 2025** book for adults and teens, as well as free downloads, at **FoursquarePrayer.org**.